DOWNY WOODPECKER

Tom Jackson

Grolier
an imprint of
■SCHOLASTIC
www.scholastic.com/librarypublishing

Published 2008 by Grolier
An imprint of Scholastic Library Publishing
Old Sherman Turnpike, Danbury,
Connecticut 06816

For The Brown Reference Group plc
Project Editor: Jolyon Goddard
Copy-editors: Lesley Ellis, Lisa Hughes,
    Wendy Horobin
Picture Researcher: Clare Newman
Designers: Jeni Child, Lynne Ross,
    Sarah Williams
Managing Editor: Bridget Giles

Volume ISBN-13: 978-0-7172-6254-0
Volume ISBN-10: 0-7172-6254-5

**Library of Congress
Cataloging-in-Publication Data**

Nature's children. Set 2.
    p. cm.
    Includes bibliographical references and
index.
    ISBN-13: 978-0-7172-8081-0
    ISBN-10: 0-7172-8081-0
    I. Animals--Encyclopedias, Juvenile. I.
Grolier (Firm)
QL49.N383 2007
590--dc22
                        2007026928

Printed and bound in China

PICTURE CREDITS

Front Cover: **Ardea**: Jim Zipp.

Back Cover: **Nature PL**: Rolf Nussbaumer;
Photolibrary.com: Don Enger;
Photos.com; **Still Pictures**: Charles O.
Slavens.

Alamy: Gay Bumgarner 18, 33, Dan
Creighton 37; **Ardea**: Tom and Pat Leeson 6,
Jim Zipp 5; Natural Visions: Ian Tait 21;
NHPA: John Shaw 26–27;
Photolibrary.com: Don Enger 22, Robert
Lubeck 2 Robert Servrancky 34;
Photos.com: 41, 42; **Shutterstock**: Tony
Campbell 17, 38, Florida Stock 10, Robert
Hambley 2–3, 14, Daniel Hebert 46, Bruce
MacQueen 4, 30, Tim Zurowski 9, 13; **Still
Pictures**: Charles O. Slavens 45.

Contents

FACT FILE: Downy Woodpecker

Class	Birds (Aves)
Order	Piciformes; includes honeyguides, woodpeckers, and toucans
Family	Woodpeckers, piculets, and wrynecks (Picidae)
Genus	*Dendrocopos*
Species	Downy woodpecker (*Dendrocopos pubescens*)
World distribution	North America
Habitat	Gardens, orchards, and woodlands
Distinctive physical characteristics	Smallest woodpecker in North America; sharp, pointed beak; white back and belly; black wings with white stripes; red spot on the head of the male
Habits	Mates for life; communicates and finds food by tapping; nests in holes in dead trees; lays four or five eggs at a time
Diet	Insects and some plants

Introduction

Woodlands are quiet places. There are few sounds other than the leaves rustling in the breeze. But a little black-and-white bird with a sharp, pointed beak can soon have a quiet woodland sounding more like a drum solo. Meet the downy woodpecker. The noise it makes results from the woodpecker rapping its beak into the bark of a tree. The downy woodpecker might be "drumming" for various reasons. It might be boring out a **nesting hole** to raise its young, searching for food—**insects** that live under the bark—or communicating with other downy woodpeckers in the forest.

The downy woodpecker is the most common woodpecker in North America.

This young downy woodpecker has just learned to fly. It can now look for food on its own.

Don't Fall!

A hungry young woodpecker must wait in the nest—in a hole dug into a dead tree—for the parent birds to bring it food. Sometimes it is a long wait. The chick sits at the entrance to the nest, waiting for its parents.

When downy woodpecker chicks hatch, they do not have feathers. Within three weeks the chick has not only grown soft downy feathers, but also the strong wing and tail feathers that it needs to be able to fly. At this point, it has yet to try them in flight. But it does not have long to wait. When the chick becomes impatient it might decide to seek out food for itself. If it sees a bug crawling past the hole of the trunk it might reach for it. This is usually the bird's first lesson in flying. As the young bird tumbles out of the tree, it tries out its wings for the first time. The young woodpecker flutters safely to the ground—it can fly!

Hello Downy

Downy woodpeckers are the smallest woodpeckers in North America. An adult downy woodpecker weighs just 1 ounce (28 g). That is about the same as an AA battery. The downy woodpecker is 6 inches (15 cm) long from the tip of its tail to its bill, or beak.

Downy woodpeckers have interesting **markings**. Most of the downy's feathers are black and white. The breast is covered in small white feathers. The wings are mainly black, but there are several rows of white dots. There is also a white stripe down the back. Males are easy to tell apart from females because they have a red patch on the top of their head.

The male downy woodpecker's red patch on its head helps it attract a mate.

The red-bellied woodpecker lives in North America. Its range covers southern Canada and the eastern United States, as far south as Florida.

Meet the Relatives

You are more likely to see a downy than any other woodpecker in North America. They live in just about all types of habitats, from woodlands and gardens to cities. But downy woodpeckers are just one of 22 North American woodpecker **species**, or types. There are an additional 156 species living in other parts of the world.

All woodpeckers are expert climbers. They have a long beak for digging out food and for drilling holes in wood. However, that is where the similarities among the different species end. Some are as small as sparrows, while others are as large as pigeons. Some woodpeckers are black and white, like the downy, but most are more brightly colored. Woodpeckers are usually insect eaters, but they also eat other food. Some woodpeckers drill into tree trunks and drink the sap that leaks out. Other woodpeckers use their tough beak to crack open acorns and other nuts.

Two of a Kind

There is another American woodpecker that looks almost the same as the downy. This species is called the hairy woodpecker. It has the same black-and-white **plumage** as the downy, and the males even have a red patch on the head, too. Scientists are not sure why the two species look the same—perhaps they are pretending to be each other. If they were perched side by side, you would see that the hairy woodpecker is much bigger than the downy. If they are not side by side, however, it is difficult to distinguish a downy woodpecker from a hairy woodpecker. The best way to tell which woodpecker is which is to look at the beak. Like most woodpeckers, the hairy woodpecker has a long beak—as long as the length of its head. However, the downy woodpecker's is short and stubby—much shorter than the length of its head.

The hairy woodpecker will sometimes eat unguarded downy woodpecker eggs.

13

A downy woodpecker's home range can vary from 1/100 to 1/20 of a square mile (0.02–0.12 sq km).

Woodpecker's Patch

Wherever they live—in your backyard, the park, or in the middle of a wild forest—each downy woodpecker defends an area called a **home range**. The bird finds all the food it needs inside the home range. This area is also filled with places to take shelter and build nests.

Downy woodpeckers like to live in areas with deciduous trees. Those are trees that drop their leaves in fall and grow them again in spring. These trees harbor the insects eaten by the woodpeckers. When the trees die, they make ideal places for the woodpeckers to drill nesting holes to sleep in or raise their chicks. Dead wood is softer and easier to drill than live wood.

In spring and summer, a male and female woodpecker share a home range. There they help each other look after their young. In fall, the pair separates, and the birds spend the rest of the year on their own. Some downy woodpeckers stay in the same home range for their whole life.

Sharing the Tree

During the cold days of fall and winter, downy woodpeckers look for food by themselves. But they do not mind sharing their home range with other birds. Sometimes two downy woodpeckers will meet at a tree. They are not competing to find precious food for their chicks at this time of year, so the two birds leave each other alone.

Downy woodpeckers often live alongside hairy woodpeckers. Sometimes these unlikely couples share the same tree, although they are usually in different parts of it. The two species eat different food, so they do not get in each other's way. Downy woodpeckers dig through the loose bark of dead branches. The larger and stronger hairy woodpeckers gouge holes in the harder, living wood of the tree trunk.

However, when spring comes, and the downy woodpeckers pair up again, visitors to the home range are no longer welcome. The downy woodpeckers will then drive other birds out of the area.

A downy woodpecker searches for grubs under the bark of a tree.

17

Holly berries, which are poisonous to humans, make a tasty winter meal for a downy woodpecker.

Downy Dinner

A downy's favorite foods are insects, such as ants and beetles. The insects scurry around on the trees and the downy has to be quick to catch them in its snappy beak. Spring and summer are the best times to catch adult insects. In winter, downy woodpeckers eat more young insects, called **larvae**. Caterpillars are the larvae of moths and butterflies, while beetle larvae are chubby, wormlike grubs. Many of these larvae live under the bark of trees, and the woodpecker chips away at the bark with its beak to get at the food underneath.

A downy woodpecker also eats fruit, such as blackberries and cherries. In winter there are not many insects around, so downy woodpeckers eat more berries. They also sip the sweet sap that oozes through the bark where larger woodpeckers have tapped deep holes into the tree trunks.

Tap, Tap, Tap

The downy woodpecker drills holes in soft, dead wood—it even digs into telephone poles! Its beak is too small to tap into harder, living wood.

The insect larvae it feeds on live in tunnels just below the surface of the wood. So, the woodpecker hammers its hard beak into the tree, over and over again to break into the tunnels. It then uses its tongue to lick out the larvae. Its tongue is long enough to poke deep into the tunnels. The tip of its tongue is covered in tiny, hooklike barbs, which help the tongue grab onto prey. The tongue is also sticky, which helps to hold on to prey, too. When not in use, the long tongue is coiled up inside the bird's mouth.

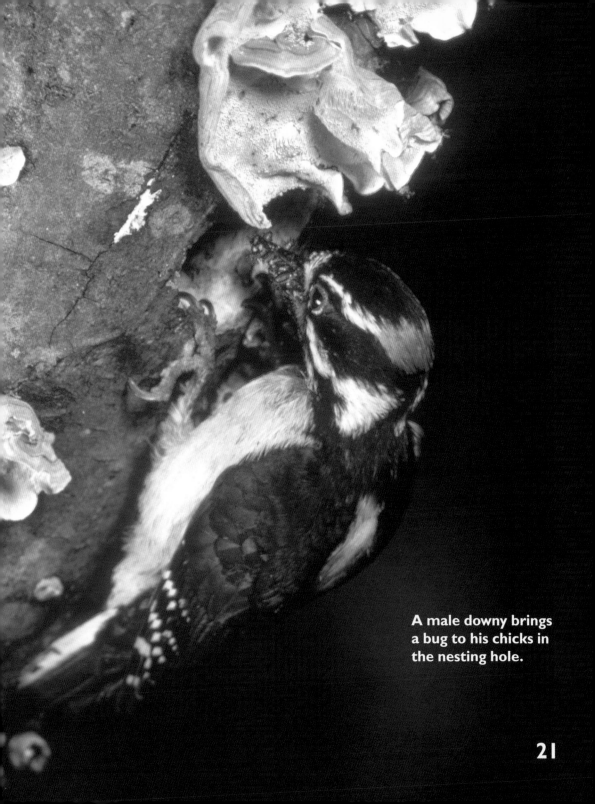

A male downy brings a bug to his chicks in the nesting hole.

21

A strong, thick beak and skull ensure that this downy woodpecker does not hurt itself while drilling.

22

Knock on Wood

No one likes banging their head, so what must it be like to be a woodpecker? When it is drilling, a woodpecker can hit its beak into the wood about 100 times a minute. But the bird does not get hurt. The hard beak is wide at the base where it connects to the skull. The skull is also thick and covered in strong muscles. Together, the wide beak, tough skull, and strong muscles absorb the shock of hitting the wood, so no damage is done.

Cutting up wood makes a lot of sawdust. People working in sawmills wear masks to stop themselves from breathing it in. Downy woodpeckers do a similar sort of thing. The **nostrils** at the base of their beak are covered in fine feathers. These feathers stop the wood dust from getting inside the bird's airway.

Getting a Grip

Downy woodpeckers like to feed at the top of
trees, where the branches are thin. They need
to be skillful climbers to stay safe up there.
They can always fly to safety if they fall. But
the birds need to be on their feet if they are
to catch anything to eat.

All woodpeckers can walk straight up tree
trunks. They have four long toes on each foot;
two toes point forward and two backward. Each
toe is tipped with a sharp, curved claw. The
claws can dig into the bark, which helps give the
bird excellent grip. The downy woodpecker also
props itself up with its tail, which can act like
a third leg. The tail is made from stiff feathers
that do not bend when the bird leans on it.

Preen and Clean

It's not all work for the downy woodpecker. Each bird has a favorite perch somewhere high up in its home range, where it takes time out now and then. While resting, the woodpecker likes nothing better than to **preen** itself. Preening is the way in which a bird keeps clean. The bird pokes its long beak deep into its feathers, wiping away any dirt or parasites. It then straightens out all the feathers again by running its beak through each one. Straightened feathers are absolutely essential for flying.

Despite all this cleaning, the feathers still get a bit ragged. Every year downy woodpeckers replace all their feathers. This process, called **molting**, takes place in summer. The old feathers fall out and are replaced by new ones. The molt takes place gradually over several weeks—the feathers do not fall out all at once. Without them the woodpecker could not fly!

A sharp, curved claw
on each toe helps this
downy woodpecker
grip an old tree trunk.

26

Heading South

Most downy woodpeckers stay at home in winter. They shelter inside deep tree holes when the weather gets cold. However, some downy woodpeckers live in places that become too cold for them in winter. Insects do not like the cold either. Without insect food, downy woodpeckers simply cannot survive.

In fall these birds fly off to spend winter in less chilly surroundings. In spring they fly home again. A seasonal journey like that is called a **migration**. Some birds migrate down mountainsides from the high forests to winter in the warmer valleys. Other birds fly many miles south, where the weather is much warmer.

To survive winter, this female downy woodpecker might stay inside a hollow branch or fly south to warmer regions.

29

Downy woodpeckers
like to soak up the
sun on a warm day.

Bath Time

Downy woodpeckers do not like getting wet. They stay in a **roosting hole** during heavy rainfall and never take a dip in pools of water. They sometimes wash with snow, however. In late winter, when the days are getting longer and warmer as spring approaches, downy woodpeckers make the most of the deep snow. They scoop up snow with their beak and fling it over their back, flapping their wings around to give themselves an early spring cleaning.

A downy woodpecker's favorite kind of bathing is sunbathing. On a hot day, you might find one of these birds sprawled facedown on a sunny branch. It will then hold its wings half open and raise the feathers on its neck to soak up the warmth of the sun.

Chit Chat

Woodpeckers are not songbirds, like robins. Breeding partners do not chirr sweetly to each other from the branches. However, they do use calls to communicate with each other. They also send messages using body movements.

When a downy is saying, "Look at me," it lets out a loud "thuck" call, which can be heard a long way off among the trees. When it is worried about something, it warns others of its type by saying "Tick-tick-tick." If danger is very close, the bird shouts "Tickirr" before flying away to safety. When the bird is relaxed, it says "Tutu-tit-wi-tut-it" to its breeding partner.

When a downy woodpecker wants to move another bird from its tree, it sends out a silent signal. It stretches up tall, points its beak into the air, and whips its head from side to side. The message is clear: "Go away!"

A downy woodpecker
will use particular body
movements to scare
off other birds from
a favorite feeding tree.

Late winter and spring are the best times to hear downies tapping, or drumming, out messages with their beak on wood.

Morse Code

Tapping on wood can make a loud noise. Downy woodpeckers sometimes drum out messages on stumps of dead wood. The noise can be heard from a long way away. The bird uses these noises to attract a **mate** or to tell other downy woodpeckers where its home range is.

The message is made up of a series of short bursts of tapping, similar to the idea of Morse code. Each burst has about 10 taps in it and lasts a couple of seconds. Then there is a short pause for a second or two before the drumming continues. To another woodpecker the drumming means, "I'm over here."

Strut and Drum

Downy woodpeckers begin to think about raising a family in late winter. The female starts to look for a mate. She drums out her message and waits for a male nearby to drum back in reply. The pair then spends a while drumming to each other. They also show off to each other by strutting along a branch with their feathers fluffed out. This period of courtship allows the birds to see whether or not their intended partner is the best one in the area. If they are sure that they have met their ideal partner, the pair then mates for life.

They usually set up home in the male's home range. The female heads back to her home range in fall. The following year the same pair goes through the courtship process again, ready to raise more chicks.

The female downy usually selects which branch to make a nesting hole.

Strong head and
neck muscles
support the
downy's chisel-
like beak when
it bores out
a nesting hole.

38

Building a Nest

A pair of a downy woodpeckers drills a new nesting hole each year. The female chooses a spot on a dead tree trunk or branch, high above the ground. The male does most of the drilling. He chisels out a cone-shaped entrance and digs down to make a deep hole. As the nest gets deeper, he must wriggle out backward to throw out the chips of wood. It takes around two weeks to finish the nesting hole.

The nest will keep the chicks warm and safe. The small entrance is only big enough to let an adult downy woodpecker through. Most **predators** are stuck outside. From the door, a passage leads down to a nesting hole, which is lined with a few soft flakes of wood.

In between digging, the woodpeckers drum out messages to make sure all the other birds in the area know to whom the nest belongs.

The Eggs Arrive

Most birds' eggs are mottled and speckled. They are patterned to make them harder to see in the nest. A downy female's eggs are laid out of sight in a snug nesting hole. As a result, no patterns on the eggs are needed. The eggs are a bright white. A female usually lays around four or five eggs each year. It takes about five days for all the eggs to be laid. After that, the woodpecker pair takes turns sitting on the eggs. That keeps the eggs warm and safe as the chicks grow inside. After about 12 days, the eggs are ready to hatch.

If food is plentiful
and the weather
favorable, a pair of
downies might raise
more than one brood
of chicks in the
breeding season.

A female downy woodpecker feeds a male chick. Young males have a red patch on the front —rather than back— of their head.

Raising a Family

Downy woodpecker **nestlings** have no feathers when they hatch. Their eyes are also tightly shut. The parents take turns bringing food to the chicks. One parent bird flies off to find some insects, while the other stays with the chicks, comforting them with soft calls.

The chicks are fed ants and other tiny insects. The parents arrive with food every two or three minutes and feed one chick at a time. To start with, the parent must put the food into each youngster's mouth. After a week or so, the chicks are strong enough to climb up from the nest to meet their parents. By now, they are eating larger insects. Before too long, the downy woodpecker chicks are crowding around the entrance, waiting for their next meal.

At night, the father stays with the chicks while their mother rests in another roosting hole. The father is in charge of keeping the nest clean. He picks up the babies' droppings in his mouth and dumps them outside.

Reach for the Sky

By three weeks old, the chicks are almost as big as their parents. The nest is getting crowded. So, the chicks start to spend time out of the nest to get a bit more space. The parents don't have to feed the chicks as much as they used to and are now able to take an occasional rest. They now feed the chicks every 20 minutes or so.

Despite still looking fairly fluffy with their baby feathers, their wings are ready for flight. The hungry chicks soon take to the air to find food themselves. Chicks that have just learned to fly are called fledglings. From now on the young flying birds will regularly preen themselves to keep their flight feathers clean and tidy.

Some female
downies do not
raise their own
chicks but help
other pairs raise
their chicks.

45

Downy woodpeckers
are solitary outside
the breeding season.
However, sometimes
they search for food
in groups.

Flying Away

Once a young downy woodpecker has flown the nest, it never comes back again. Each one finds a place to sleep among the leaves of a nearby tree. It is summer now, so the young birds do not get too cold. They can climb well and they are getting better at flying all the time. But they still need help finding food. Their mother and father provide them with tidbits, tracking down each chick by their loud calls. The youngster with the loudest call gets fed first.

Gradually the family begins to get spread out as the young birds travel farther apart to find food. By the middle of summer, the birds are fully grown. They fly off to set up their own home range. They spend winter alone, just as older birds do. In spring it will be time for them to search for a mate.

Tough, Old Bird

Once a downy woodpecker reaches adulthood, it can look forward to a long life. It has survived its childhood, which is the most dangerous period of its life. It could have been killed as an egg or in the nest by a small predator, such as a red squirrel. While it flapped around during its first few days out of the nest, the young woodpecker was also at risk of attack by hawks and other hunting birds.

Adult downy woodpeckers do not have many enemies and they have everything they need to survive—their tough drilling beak. A downy woodpecker is likely to live for eight or nine years and raise many chicks along the way.

Words to Know

Home range   An area that an animal or group of animals lives in.

Insects   Animals with six legs and a body made of three parts. Many insects also have wings. They include flies, beetles, wasps, and bugs.

Larvae   The second stage of an insect's life, after it has hatched out of the egg.

Markings   Patterns and colors in fur and feathers.

Mate   Either member of an animal pair; to come together to produce young.

Migration   A journey made each year to find a place to feed, mate, or give birth.

Molting   To shed feathers or fur from time to time.

Nesting hole	A hole dug in trees by a downy woodpecker to make a nest.
Nestlings	Young birds that have not yet left the nest.
Nostrils	Openings in the nose or beak that allow air into and out of the body.
Plumage	The feathers of a bird.
Predators	Hunting animals that kill other animals for food.
Preen	To groom feathers with the beak.
Roosting hole	A hole in a tree where a downy woodpecker sleeps at night.
Species	The scientific word for animals of the same type that can breed together.

Find Out More

Books

Backhouse, F. *Woodpeckers of North America*. Toronto: Firefly Books, 2005.

Mania, C. and R. C. Mania Jr. *Woodpeckers in the Backyard*. Wildlife Conservation Society Books. London, UK: Franklin Watts, 2000.

Web sites

Cornell Laboratory
www.birds.cornell.edu/BOW/DOWP/
Many facts about downy woodpeckers.

U.S. Geological Survey—Downy Woodpeckers
www.mbr-pwrc.usgs.gov/Infocenter/i3940id.html
Includes photographs, songs, videos, identification tips, maps, and other useful information.

Index